Autumn Eyes

Autumn Eyes

20 Poems

&

One Short Story

Craig D. Smith

With

Nancy A. Smith

Graphics Design: Craig D. Smith
Author Photos: Laura J. Tenny
First publication: December 2025

Library of Congress Cataloging-in-publication Data
Smith, Craig D. (Craig Donald), 1949 –

Autumn Eyes / Craig D. Smith
Published, 2025
ISBN: 9798269917375
Imprint: Independently published

Printed in the United States of America

Dedication

For Candy and Jenny - who wait for me.
For Mom and Dad – Always
For my dear Laura

Acknowledgements

Much appreciation goes to those who encourage my writing.

My friend Bob Olsen - Since we were in High School,
Ken & Sandy Turney - Always with good words and advice
Laura Tenny - Who keeps my grammar (mostly) correct.
Susan Hornung – Who always gives good and honest input

I am also continually grateful to friends Ken and Judy, whose
beach house regularly provides me a place to write.

TABLE OF CONTENTS

FORWARD

This marks my fifth collection of "twenty poems and one short story"—a format I've come to call "twenty-and-one" books. While these smaller volumes began as side projects during work on longer pieces, they've become something I genuinely treasure. After completing the fourth book, "Facing the Waters," I told myself it would be the last. Then I found various pieces written by my sister Nancy, who died suddenly in 2012.

As I read through her work—I can't quite recall how they all came into my hands—I realized they deserved a wider audience. "Autumn Eyes" brings together ten of Nancy's poems and her memoir "I Remember Grandma," interwoven with some of my own writing.

Nancy had a talent for noticing what truly matters: small gestures, everyday rituals, and the feelings we carry from childhood into adulthood. She captures many of the sensory details that make memories vivid and real. For example, in "Going to the Fair," she describes returning home late from that activity when our mom would wipe our hands and sleepy faces with washcloths before sending us to bed. That scene brought back the sensation of a warm washcloth against tired skin and heavy eyelids after hours of excitement. She also perfectly captures the thrill of Dad rocking our Ferris wheel seat at its highest point.

How do these pieces relate to Autumn?

Autumn naturally invites reflection—on memories, thoughts, and emotions that surface as we slow down with *the changing leaves and seasons, that space between summer's warmth and winter's silence. This transition prompts us to consider our place under God's heaven and the good, merciful, humorous, and even strange things we experience in life, including how love is measured through sadness, loss, and grief.*

A reflective and sincere quality of observation hopefully color these pages. The poems drift between romance and childhood memories, from wandering thoughts to reflections on life's endings and how love deepens over time. Here are remembrances, contemplations of mortality and pain, celebrations of what was—and what endures.

Life's colors seen through Autumn eyes.

Autumn Eyes

EMBERS AND EMBRACES

Autumn Eyes

Meteor Time 1967

Straw bales lined up in the field -
That place behind your house, where we watched the sky,
Away from the city,
Away, where darkness wrapped the night.

With a blanket beneath us, around us,
Embracing us alone - except for the heavens above -
Stars were loosened and fell like discarded jewels.

Streaking across the heavens - they landed on…you,
To make you gently glow in the blue-black night.
You didn't notice them surrounding you,

But that was all I could see.

Craig Smith
November 2019

Slow Dance

I was so cruel, I know I broke your heart.
Reckless and unkind, I tore our love apart.
I live in silent sadness; I have no words to say.
I know how much I hurt you; I pushed your love away.

Oh, take my hand… take my hand.
In a slow dance.
Again, my love… oh my love.
In a slow dance.

Foolishly, I lost you; I turned away from you.
But found that I still love you, don't you know it's true!
You know how much I'm hoping, don't tell me you can't see.
Please, my love, forgive me! Can you come back to me?

Oh, take my hand… take my hand.
In a slow dance.
Come back to me… back to me.
In a slow dance.

Don't leave me crying; please let me feel you near.
I cannot live without you; return to me, my dear.
I'll wrap my arms around you. Please know that I will stay.
I'll be yours forever, until our final day.

Oh, take my hand… take my hand.
In a slow dance.
Forever yours… I am yours.
In a slow dance.

In a slow dance.
In a slow dance.

Craig Smith
July 2024

Autumn Eyes

Burnt River

I lost my love on Burnt River —
In that fire that wrapped us around.
For I learned only one was the giver,
And dear love, you took me down.

For I thought I'd be livin' and dyin',
By that river that stole you away.
You said we'd grow old there together,
Burnt River would not let you stay.

Burnt River has left me aloneness,
Its waters flow past deep and wide.
I can't speak your name near that river,
The sorrow just tears me inside.

Oh, I lost my love on Burnt River.
As its waters claimed you that day.
For the call of its name,
Carried you far away,
In a boat on its river of flame.

.

Nancy Ann Smith
March 2000

The Scapular

On soft brown ropes
it hung there, holy -
with the Mother of God
watching over.

It was a secret thing.

Hiding under blouses, unknown to everyone,
but... comforting, brushing against my skin -
The Sisters said if you died within its arms
that Mary lifted you straight to Jesus.

Later, older,
believing that you loved me was my scapular.
You, lying there between the beats of my heart,
that lovely secret.

And each day I examined the shape of it.
(Underneath where no one else could see),
A roughness that trembled on my breast like a shiver,
within which I was never alone.

Now without you,
I feel so unholy, naked, and if I should die,
I fear there would be nothing left of me
to rise up to the Mother of God.

Nancy Ann Smith
February 1995

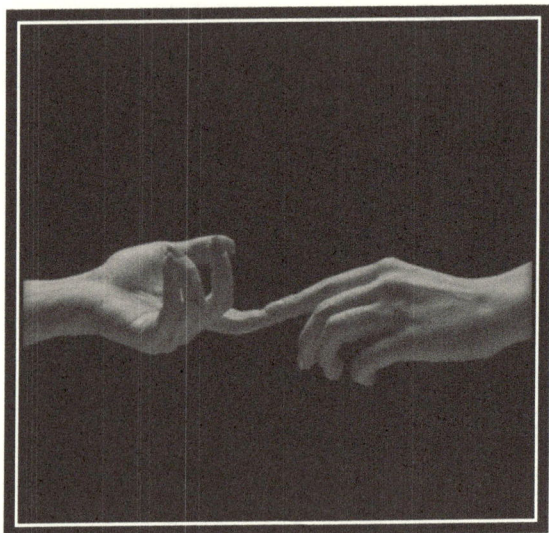

Turning Points

There is a blended moment that I've seen with you and I, where things like time and wounds and scars are mixed between our eyes.

And only these things matter there, and nothing is concealed; Of love and death, and growth of life from seeds, our choices sealed.

No whispers of the outside world can pierce that subtle veil; No reality of daily things may touch, or cry, or wail. But from within that lonely instant, I find I am among the unexpected reveries of someone I could love.

This thought secretly entraps me, and I pause to pull it back. My emotions become entangled; my will starts growing slack. I know I have betrayed you as the bond between us flies, and I think that you have sensed the change, as my conversation dies.

And I want to cry "forgive me", that I've burdened you with that part, and imagined you the answer to a solitary heart.

Craig Smith
May 1998

Autumn Eyes

MOMENTS HELD

Going to the Fair

When I was a child
On a hot July evening full of deep maple shadows,
We kids would sit on pins and needles on our porch
To watch for Daddy's red truck to turn down our street.

Grabbing his lunch pail and two fingers,
We would drag him into Mother …
Because we were going to the fair.

The park was filled with people.
And the trees moved easily overhead.
Less easily than we moved!
Dancing on the end of imaginary leashes, wanting to be off…

Mom would wrap up our coins in knotted handkerchiefs
Where they weighed heavily in our hands -
Silver dimes and nickels begging to be spent
To buy some brightly colored toys or souvenirs.

And every year we waited with happy
Screams just tucked inside our mouths,
For Daddy to rock the Ferris Wheel seat…
Back and forth, back and forth,
Just when we hit the top.

Finally, sated like royalty on snow cones and cotton candy,
We would drive home in our old green Chevy,
And Mom would take washcloths to our hands
And sleepy faces, and send us off to bed.

Oh, now to be able to just open our hands, to show a child
How to wrap up such magic and memories
In knotted handkerchiefs -
To put aside for days when they are no longer young.

Nancy Ann Smith
August 2011

15

Mother's Day

If I could have chosen while I blossomed
Cell by cell inside you -
Like a lilac unfolding petal by petal,
Woven into the mayday crown you made for me,
So that I could walk in white patent leather shoes
Down holy aisles to honor our Holy Mother.

If I could have prayed
For a thousand whisper-robed archangels
In grey pussywillow wings
To drift God's golden dust of grace upon me,

I could not have asked for a greater heart
To raise me up.

So, since there are surely
Lilacs and archangels in majesty,
Soft-winged in pussywillows -
Watching over me.

Then surely God
intended you… to be my mother.

Nancy Ann Smith
May 1989

17

Balance

Training wheels. Yes. I needed them,
Wobbly side to side and tipping over too -
Scraped knees and mostly scared to try to ride alone.

But I remember the day,
We took the training wheels away.
(I'm sure you don't, but I remember!)

Down the block from our house,
With Mom watching
I was scared and unsure.

Dad had his hand on the seat of my bike
Telling me he wouldn't let me fall
As I pedaled toward home.

So, in that first (of many) leaps of faith
I struck out and away
On my pink and white Schwinn.

I was sure that Dad was still holding on
(How else could I still be upright?)
I looked back, astonished.

Dad smiling at me a half a block behind.
Mom smiling at me a half a block ahead.

Balance.

Nancy Ann Smith
December 2003

Garden of Remembering

Why is it now we all gravitate homeward
One by one, like planets in decreasing orbit,
To where we bury our friends, the well-loved
Dogs, cats and animals of our childhood-no-longer?

When we were small, we traipsed with Daddy and a shovel
Into this hallowed part of the garden.
Here we laid our pets to rest with many tears,
And memories of soft fur and warm eyes.

And now, even now - grown,
We can still point out the fading markers to others
Like milestones to our growth.

And we still walk, alone or with husbands,
Wives or children, in sorrowful procession
Carrying boxes of quiet love…

To plant them in our parents'
Garden of remembering.

Nancy Ann Smith
January 1986

21

Ada's Funeral

The rituals of living and dying
Surprise me now as I find myself
No longer young.

Funeral attendance once dreaded
Now becomes a necessary obligation.
It ties me to the group whose blood,
Like mine, share the features and traits
Of those we love.

Today we buried my mother's aunt.
My grandmother's brother's wife.
I played on their farm when I was eight or so.
I played with their children, so far beyond me.
They were teenagers, and I was not.
I played with their cows and chickens, and horses,
The dogs, the kittens…

Autumn Eyes

My Uncle Joe and Aunt Ada
Were always comfortable to have gangs of children
Roaming over.

Thirty-six years later, I have not seen
Those distant cousins, far flung now,
Nor even exchanged a lonely Christmas card.

Yet we come, all together, to bury their mother.
And I grieve their loss, the one we all pray not to have -
"Not now, Lord, maybe later - ten, twenty years; later."
Never late enough for that chasm of absence.

But Ada, in her full span of years,
Told us at her death, she went forward to her husband-
"Joe? Joe!"- before she breathed her last.

And the years fall away before common parents,
Grandparents, aunts, and uncles.
But we stand with each other as children still.

And as we impose our hands over
The casket of their mother,
We hold each other in unseen ways
However distant,
Because we are part of that elusive
But tensile web we call family.

Nancy Ann Smith
October 1980

Augusta's Garden

Augusta's Garden grew wild
in front of her rickety house on Oak Street.
On hot September afternoons
I would pass it walking home from kindergarten,
I being no taller than the rosebushes there.

It was so still -
I could lay my cheek on the quiet sidewalk
to feel its warmth and listen to the crickets in the grass.
There was only a simple wooden sign
in front of the old cottage, it read "Augusta's Garden."
That sign introduced me to her.

But I never saw her weeding, you know,
nor spraying, spading, tilling.
Yet what a wild profusion grew from her hands!
Roses, dahlias, sunflowers, snapdragons, foxglove -
Pink and violet, yellow and red
Springing from the good deep,
Rich and wise soil of her soul.

Augusta would smile, and I would smile.
But I never knew her beyond that smile and her flowers.
She would sit on her porch in the shade.
Surely, she was willing her garden to grow.
I was just another homeward-bound child.

So why am I now so bereft?
Her cottage and garden are bulldozed away.
Only a struggling rose breaks the dust
where the rambling garden once flowered
to bless a homeward child.

Nancy Ann Smith
August 1990

25

Autumn Eyes

WHISPERS AND MUSINGS

The Slow Unraveling

The leaves know something we pretend not to—
how easy it is to let go,
how the branches don't beg them to stay.

October light slants through bare places
where green once was,
and the air tastes of smoke and ending things.

I walk through drifts of rust and amber,
each step a small burial,
the season performing its quiet demolition.

The trees stand like skeletons at a funeral
for their own flesh, graceful in their grief,
dressed in the colors of dying well.

Everything beautiful is leaving.
The geese write their goodbyes across the sky
in languages we've forgotten how to read.

Soon the world will be stripped down
to its bones — gray branches against grayer sky,
the earth hard and honest beneath our feet.

But for now, in this in-between,
the wind carries the scent of apples rotting sweetly,
and I am neither here nor already gone,

I am just another thing learning how to fall.

Craig Smith
October 2010

The Moon Laments

What liar said,
The moon smiles?

If you look at the moon
With your eyes peeled of dreams,
Then you will know the moon
As she is.

With half-smiling irony and brows up-slanted -
Like a tragedy in a white columned round.

There she hangs, like a host beneath a blue ciborium.
And with agony in the night sky garden,
She knows, like He who would come after,
Too much about the hearts of men.

So do not sing me songs of love.
Do not lie to me
While she sits behind the clouds!
For I know (though you may not yet see).

The Moon
The Moon

Laments.

Nancy Ann Smith
August 2010

The Good Samaritan

He fell down in the middle of the street -
Hard on unforgiving asphalt.
He lived in the nursing home next to my grandma's house,
A child inside; a simple-minded, ruby-cheeked man,
With always a wordless moon-wide smile as he shuffled by.

I stopped to help him.

And so did Red Beard,
A man with an open fly,
Passing by the scene,
Stinking of beer.

The fallen man of course, wasn't drunk,
Only simple, unsteady, old, confused, startled,
And rising, he began to shake my hand -
Again, and again…
up and down,
Again and again,
up and down, to thank me.

So, I resumed travel to my appointed destination,
Leaving behind just thirty seconds of my day, where he fell.

Red Beard helped him to the curb.
He picked up scattered change lost in the fall,
And returned it to the man's grey coveralls.
Then brushing him off,
Red Beard began to guide the fallen traveler home.

Was it You who fell on that unforgiving asphalt?
You… the least of us all?
Will Red Beard ask "Oh, Lord, when was it You?"

And who do you suppose was the good Samaritan?

Nancy Ann Smith
June 1989

A Place in Hopewell

Have you found a place in Hopewell town?
For I am journeying home,
Walking along this quiet road, through drifts of snow.
I'll look to find you waiting.

I'll see you soon in Hopewell.
Just stand out on our porch.
I'll know it's you. Oh! Please wave to me.
I do want in from this cold.

I so want to be home in Hopewell,
I know we'll all be there,
Together once more with joy again.
We'll be warm there by the fire.

I'll be there soon in Hopewell.
I really won't be long.
And minutes pass like heartbeats -
Running slowly down…

Toward a gentle reunion.

Craig Smith
October 1995

Autumn Eyes

THROUGH AUTUMN EYES

The Playhouse

Jenny Smith: 1980 – 1993

Today I cut into your memory,
It was a logical decision; it made sense.
It was your small room at the end of the garage.
A playhouse once finished - six by six - for you to enjoy.
One window, a door, sealed in clean sheetrock,
A place for secrets, comic books, and sleepovers with friends.

Now it sits still, with sun-faded magenta-less posters
Still taped to its white walls… left there for years.
Batman's Robin poster is now mainly green.
Your cat pictures are washed out into one color… blue.
Other things in the playhouse are mostly gone from when
You were twelve. The outer door barely opens.

This was once a secret place, but is no longer holding
Things of friends and fun.
Whispers and giggles are silent.
Walls are dusty, webbed with spiders.
It would be easier had you released it willingly,
Before your youth was stolen.

But these days, used for storage, it needs better access.
It will hold wood. It will be a repository for odd and
Meaningless overflow from the garage.
So, I need to open a wall, cut an inner door!
Just an opening to easily add the less important…
While other things that were yours - escape.

And as my anxiety slices through that wall,
With saw in hand, I say with great… great difficulty,
"This is just a door."

Craig Smith
October 2010

Morning Fog

Another day to pass through
That wakes - slow... my opening eyes,
With remnants of my yesterdays
Still tacked to unseen skies...

Cold fog floats across the morning.
It slides over longing hills,
To slowly drag my memories out,
from coffee, cold - now still.

Morning silence... how it moves me,
Morning mists as Autumn sighs.
To place my mind with frigid hand,
On stones where souls now lie.

Oh, that once more I could move again!
But not today. I cannot move today!
For the motion of one languid thought,
Might steal my life away.

Craig Smith
February 2000

41

Grieving

But I want to see her
 again.
I want to see her
 again.

Oh God, move me away,
Far away from the pain.
Lift me up past the spires of time.

Where dawn and dusk meet,
And blend in defeat,
Into this hushed sorrow of mine.

Let no morning or evening
Find me wanting of her.
Let me fly... Let me run...
Let me hide...

In an empty smile,
In a traveled mile...
From the ghosts in my mind...
When she's gone.

Craig Smith
August 1968

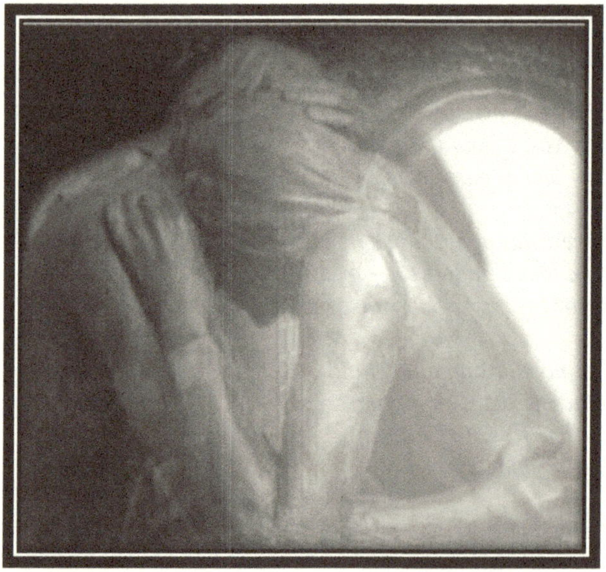

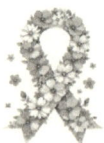

The Conversation

Candyce June Smith: 1949-1994

A day captured by pictures in a scrapbook.
These heavens have raced through our lives,
Time has crashed; life has stopped.
It is wreckage lying with photos now in the dark.

Eyes closed, quiet for a while,
It makes no difference. Your tears, my tears...
And how could there not be tears for a lost child?
Tears wash our hearts; in them we taste our lives.

And then, you talk of what I should do
After you are also gone! (How like you!)
No! That is too much to consider. How can I?
Better to just remove my heart once more.
Better to let God consume me in fire,
Rather to be ashes than this sorrow.
My garments are torn.

I think God does not touch this bubble of air
As much as our fantasies might imagine.
He has left his Breath to blow away the dust
From our lives, sometimes painfully –
To reveal the rock of our faith.

(But still, I inwardly curse!
I would try to slip inside your skin,
To replace your tumors into my own body.
Just as we would have given breath for our daughter.)

So, we talk of the shadows approaching.
Of our youth gone by... lost it seems.
We speak of children unseen, those we will never know...
And the one known.

And where she waits now, soon to see
With open eyes,
Paradise.

Craig Smith
August 1995

45

The Last Poem of Autumn

For Laura

I think of you in the middle of ordinary things—
You have become like coming home and setting out all at once.
Sometimes it's just wanting to tell you anything...
A show-and-tell about even the mundane.
I speak of things that are not worth mentioning
Which you might enjoy, though I know you will not remember.

How you've made a home in my thoughts, my heart.
You unpack your things each morning without asking
Or knowing. I expect to see your keys on my kitchen counter.
By the time I wake, you are not here but already everywhere.
I can no longer annoy you with run-on sentences,
You are my favorite plot twist I didn't see coming.

When you look at me, what you see is home.
When I look back, I understand what our songs were about.
If I say your name, you hear it as if it were my own.
You are still quiet as fog, soft-footed as dawn,
Warm as the sun. We are different yet so much the same.
But even without words we are fluent in each other...

And isn't that the trick of it!

Craig Smith
October 2025

Autumn Eyes

ONE SHORT STORY

I Remember Grandma

I remember my grandma.

I remember her kitchen—yellow, and if it was ever a different color, I never knew it. An old sink sat beneath a window that framed the backyard, where Bachelor's Buttons grew around a tree stump, their petals pink, blue, and white against the grass.

Every late summer evening, Grandma gathered fallen apples from beneath the apple tree in that backyard, cradling them in her apron as she walked back to the house.

Her kitchen smelled perpetually of apples or stews simmering on the stove with its white enamel knobs. I can still hear the tick-tick-tick of her toaster as I waited for my bread to pop, that mechanical heartbeat underscored by country-western music crackling from a beige plastic radio on the kitchen table. "Oh Grandma," I'd say, "that music is terrible," and she would laugh and tease me back.

A space beneath the toaster shelf extended back into the house (below a stairway) like a tunnel boring deep into the earth—at least that's what I liked to imagine. I remember decks of red playing cards scattered where, occasionally, I'd catch her mid-solitaire, and she had a collection of matchbooks that I pored over again and again, studying their tiny advertisements like sacred texts.

I remember Grandma teaching me to count and sing in German, her voice patient and sure.

I bought her birds—decorative ones with fake feathers for the driftwood tree she hung on the porch. There was a chair there, and on spring evenings, I'd ride my pink and white Schwinn with its basket full, catching her sitting and watching the day fade. Grandpa had died and been gone for a long time, but I never questioned whether she was happy or lonely. She was just Grandma, and that was enough.

I remember her catching ants with me, both of us crouched on the sidewalk by the back porch steps, our spoons at the ready. We built an ant kingdom on her porch, stored in jars packed with sand. I watched them tunnel and build their invisible cities, and Grandma watched them too.

Her refrigerator was always full, and visitors never went away hungry. I remember her laughter—she'd close her eyes and the sound would rise high and bright. I remember her way of sticking her tongue in her cheek when you kissed her goodbye, and how she swore at me with a rough voice full of love. Somehow, it never sounded bad in Grandma's voice.

And I remember her hands with the ring bearing four colored stones, and her pretty legs. I remember how she teased us kids with a glint in her eye.

She had prickly rose-colored couches and chairs in her living room, and green wallpaper, with greenish woodwork. I remember sitting on the floor in front of her chair on summer evenings, the front door open, a breeze filtering through the black screen door, which had a spring that groaned and always made it slam shut with a bang.

I tried to learn to knit with her, picking knitting needles by their color, Grandma didn't care even though she'd always say the number tens would be best for me. I remember my brief lessons in casting that lasted about five minutes before my attention wandered elsewhere.

She also had a treadle sewing machine where she tolerated me making my Barbie dress creations—which never quite fit—and the endless potholders I churned out.

In her dining room was a big table that became a magic cave when rain drummed against the windows. She'd hand me all the glass animals from her cabinet, and I'd imagine worlds within worlds, listening to the rain, cozy beneath the great mahogany base of that table, warmed by soft heat blowing from a nearby vent.

And Grandma had an electric organ. She played chords over and over, teaching me "How Great Thou Art" and how to use the foot pedals; her patience was endless as my fingers and feet fumbled.

There was also the piano room, where my mother, my uncles, and all of us stood, framed in pictures on doilies atop the piano. It was always cold in there, and colder still upstairs—that part of the house was no longer used. The upstairs felt shrine-like to me; steep creaking steps leading to the place where "Mother grew up," a bedroom with slanted ceilings and lace curtains, blue and deserted.

I remember Grandma walking down to my Mother's house, where she'd sit on a blanket in the front yard watching for my sisters to come home from school. Later, she was there with snacks when I walked home, when daffodils stood yellow around the maple trees. No cinnamon roll has ever tasted the way it did when I was six and she cut it into little squares.

She would weed our yard and feed our beagle Willie, never wanting to show she really liked him. I remember her at our garage sales, playing salesman to the shoppers with unsubtle hints and charm.

And Grandma would walk all over town, clipping coupons, entering contests to win us kids a bike, writing shopping lists on the backs of grocery receipts and envelopes. I remember her coming up our driveway.

And in church she would tease us until we snickered into our hymn books. I remember her rosary, her black hair, the way her shoulders curved just a little bit. I remember her calling our house, sometimes too many times a day.

I remember so much about Grandma, and yet I never thought then what I wonder now—whether she was bored, lonely, happy, or content. She was only my grandma, a silhouette I'd recognize blocks away, walking steadily home.

And I remember Grandma being sick—and how I abandoned her then. To my child's mind, she was different in hospital gowns and behind plain walls, not the same as my grandma of the ants, birds, and lilacs. I cried and bargained with God for her, and once when I did go to see her, she cried, and it shattered my little castle of grief. The walls were just too thin for a child to bear.

I remember the regret that I couldn't see her back then— that I couldn't still be the child of the sidewalk and the Schwinn bike for her. I remember I could not go to her funeral.

And now, after all these years, I find myself remembering and grieving, grieving again—but differently this time. The regret has softened at its edges. I understand now what I couldn't then: that love doesn't require perfect courage, that a child's fear in the face of death is its own kind of innocence.

In my mind, I hear her voice—rough and warm and full of that particular sass that was hers alone. "Oh, stop your blubbering," she says, laughing. "I'm waiting with an ant jar and a spoon for the little girl on the white Schwinn bike. And I always knew you loved me."

And she did know. She knew it in every bird I brought her, every moment I sat at her feet on summer evenings, every time I chose her kitchen over any other place in the world. She knew it the way grandmothers know—completely, without question, without need for proof.

I remember Grandma. And in remembering, I find her still here: in the smell of apples, in the sound of screen doors slamming, in the yellow of spring daffodils. She is the silhouette I'd recognize anywhere, walking steadily toward me across the years. And in my imagination, when she reaches me, I take her hand—weathered and warm— I tell her, "I'm still here, Grandma. I'm still the little girl on the white Schwinn bike who loves you so much."

Then we sit together in her kitchen, listening to her radio, needing to say nothing at all.

Nancy Ann Smith
Granddaughter of Genevieve Stroeder Foelker
June 1984

Autumn Eyes

Autumn Eyes

ILLUSTRATIONS AND ART:

Cover and Inside Title Plate: <u>Light in Misty Autumn Forest</u> ID 76383677 © Smileus | (Dreamstime.com License CC0-1.0)

1. **Meteor Time 1967:** © Author modified AI Generated Image

2. **Slow Dance:** <u>Couple Slow Dancing</u> – ID 93375871 © Poznyakov | (Dreamstime.com License CC0-1.0)

3. **Burnt River:** <u>River in Autumn</u> - ID 367499870 © Iryna Kushnarova | (Dreamstime.com License CC0-1.0)

4. **Turning Point:** <u>Fingers Touching</u> - ID 303183353 © Kinomaster | (Dreamstime.com License CC0-1.0)

5. **The Scapular:** <u>Woman Wearing a Scapular</u> –Author modified ID 313768897 / ID 313816767 © Stockvectorwin | (Dreamstime.com License CC0-1.0)

6. **Going to the Fair:** <u>Carnival Midway</u> – ID 93454805 © Chris Boswell | (Dreamstime.com License CC0-1.0)

7. **Mother's Day:** © Author's Collection

8. **Balance:** <u>Child Rides Bike</u> - ID 284878667 © Artsterdam | (Dreamstime.com License CC0-1.0)

9. **Garden of Remembering:** <u>Pet Collar</u> - ID 388309066 © Rosskatena | (Dreamstime.com License CC0-1.0)

10. **Ada's Funeral:** © Author's Collection

11. **Augusta's Garden:** © Author modified - AI Generated Image

12. **The Slow Unraveling:** <u>Autumn Landscape</u>- ID 151793239 © MaksimPasko | Dreamstime.com License CC0-1.0)

13. **The Moon Laments:** <u>The Moon Reflected on Lake</u> - ID 28992605 © Dary423 | (Dreamstime.com License CC0-1.0)

14. ***The Good Samaritan:*** *Good Samaritan by Van Gogh- ID 181110817 © Mrreporter |(Dreamstime.com License CC0-1.0)*

15. ***A Place in Hopewell:*** *Bridge in Hopewell, Va. Author Modified – (Public Domain)*

16. ***The Playhouse:*** *Girl at Window -ID 35146254 © Alexandr Vasilyev |(Dreamstime.com License CC0-1.0)*

17. ***Fog:*** *Foggy Forest - ID 26636934 © Péter Gudella |(Dreamstime.com License CC0-1.0)*

18. ***Grieving:*** *Depression - ID 102351067 © Jakub Krechowicz |(Dreamstime.com License CC0-1.0*

19. ***The Conversation:*** *Reconciliation Statue at Coventry Cathedral - ID 123403602 (Author Modified) © Chris Dorney|(Dreamstime.com License CC0-1.0)*

20. ***Last Poem of Autumn:*** *Young Couple Walking –(Author Modified) © David Martyn - Big Stock Photo ID 915919 | (Copyright Extended License)*

21. ***I Remember Grandma:*** *© Author's Collection*

Craig D. Smith Photos: Laura Tenny © Author's Collection
Nancy A. Smith Photos:- © Author's Collection
Family: – © Author's Collection

Autumn Eyes

ABOUT THE AUTHORS

Craig D. Smith

is a Portland, Oregon
writer who came to writing
later in life, pursuing it
seriously only after retiring
from a career at Xerox. The
science fiction and fantasy
masters of his youth —
Bradbury, Burroughs,
Verne, Heinlein, among
others — left an indelible
mark on his imagination. While his published work leans
toward speculative fiction, he has also written the book
"Everyman's War" related to WWII and his father, as well
as several scripts. Throughout it all, poetry has been a quiet
practice for years, accumulating in notebooks and files.

Nancy Ann Smith

Nancy, Craig Smith's sister,
earned her arts degree from
the University of Portland,
where she cultivated both
vocal performance and
writing abilities. Her stage
credits included musical
theatre productions such as
Sondheim's "Lovers, Liars
and Clowns," "Fiorello," and
"Jesus Christ Superstar." She later graduated with honors
from Lewis and Clark Law School in 1984 and established
her own practice in Portland.

Nancy died in 2012 after a brief illness. Her family mourns
her loss— she herself writing of loss and death, that it is
"never late enough for that chasm of absence."

61

Autumn Eyes

Autumn Eyes

AVAILABLE ON AMAZON BY CRAIG D. SMITH

Everyman's War
'The Book' (2008)
"Taut, lean, direct, unadorned, stunningly readable, this story of courage and love quietly becomes the Human Story of Courage and Love. I finished the last pages, thanked the Coherent Mercy for putting me in this bruised and blessed world, and called my dad."
~ Brian Doyle, author of
'Mink River' & 'The Plover'

Everyman's War '
The Movie' (2008)
Winner G.I. Film Festival'
One man's hope…
One man's courage…
Everyman's War.

"If I could package the mission of the GI Film Festival into one two-hour film, it would be
'Everyman's War'"
Brandon L. Millet -
President G.I. Film Festival 2008

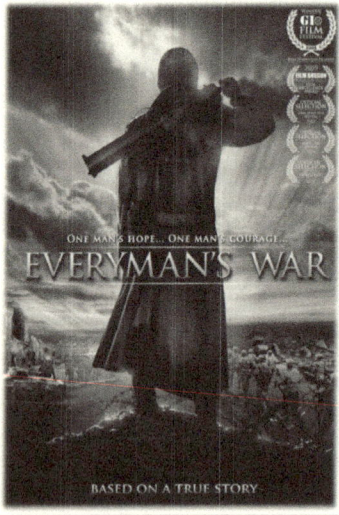

64

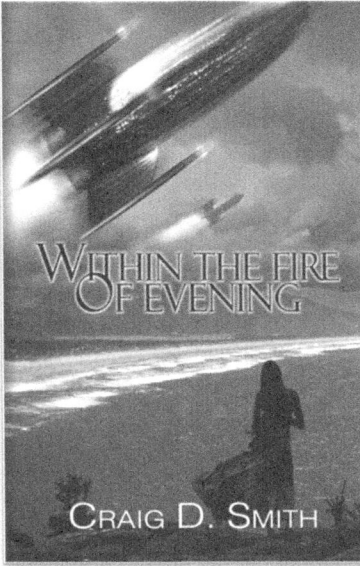

Within the Fire of Evening (2018)

"Science-fiction with a heart. It holds the glow of a warm, comforting, eerily familiar future. You will be taken to the stars...You will be taken through time. And woven through it all is a haunting yet uplifting nostalgia for days long past. The settings vary, the humanity doesn't. Here are nine tales that leave you with a yearning, "if only..."
~John Olsen, author of :
The Crystal Screen

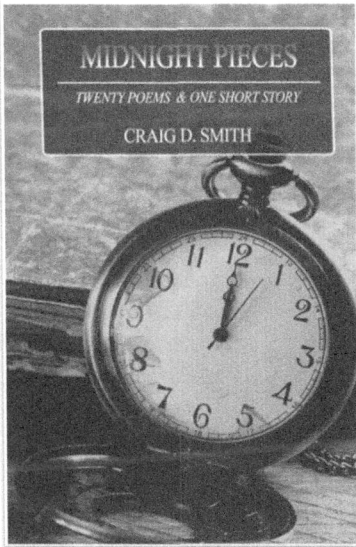

Midnight Pieces (2019)

Twenty poems and one short story. A collection of personal poetry from over the years, plus an engaging short story of romance and creativity.

"For those who encourage...
For those who edify...
For those who inspire...
And for those who know midnights..."

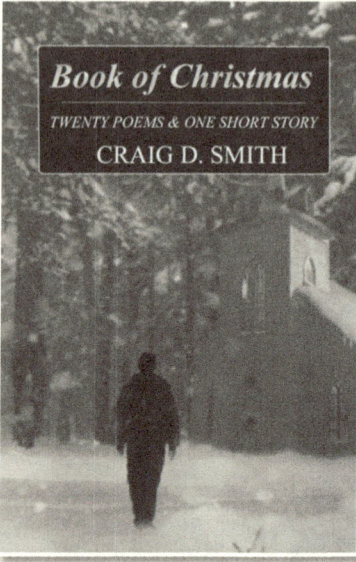

Book of Christmas (2020)
A collection of poems written over the years in various styles, which, along with the short story 'The Final Word,' directly and indirectly explore themes of nativity, ransom, restoration, and other aspects of Christmas. This book celebrates God's love and desire for us - undeserved, graciously offered, and simply obtained by saying "yes" to His gift.

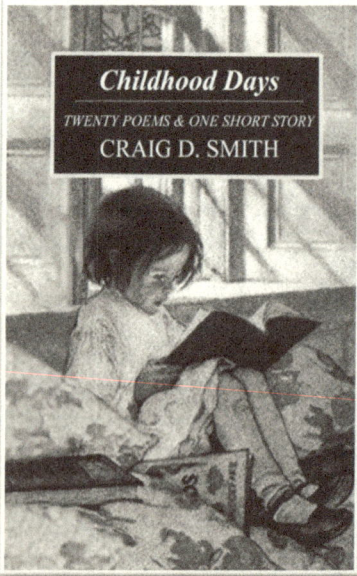

Childhood Days (2021)
Poems that speak to and about children with a simple touch of imagination, interest, and fantasy. Some poems are whimsical and humorous, while others are more serious and designed to be enjoyed by all ages. Additionally, there is a short story, an adventure exploring deeper meanings. This book is meant to bend down to a child's eye.

66

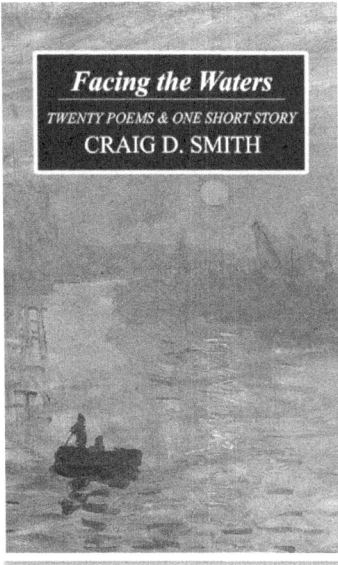

Facing the Waters (2023)

Enchantments, Lamentations, Reflections; meditations in verse like the refreshing coolness of standing in a river during a hot summer day, where water flows past stones and rocks, shaping and being shaped by them – much like life.

Facing the waters, finding many considerations in the process, interesting in form and fresh to the heart, like colorful stones from the river.

And a short story: a thoughtful interview on life and sacrifice with a soldier… a ghost.

67

Autumn Eyes

Autumn Eyes

AFTERWORDS

What do these symbols from page 'V' mean?

The symbols are from a bracelet the author often wears.

He came
He died
He arose
He ascended
He is coming again!

↘ † ◠ ↗ ↘

John 1:4

In Him was life, and that life was the light of all mankind.

The Family Smith...

Thad	Craig(me)	Nancy	Dad (Don)	Mom (Dorine)	Debbie	Lori
		D.2012	D.2019	D.2021	D.2021	

Cherry Stones — In Autumn
(Apologies to A.A. Milne)

Tinker, Sailor, Lawyer, Soldier,
Singers, Musicians, Teacher — bolder!

Not rich, not poor, no beggar or thief,
No Doctor, one Lawyer, no Indian Chief.

Oh, there are so many things we've been and tried to be.
But still, lots of cherries hang on life's cherry tree.

We've labored, and we've written, seeking to be true,
In silk or satin finery, or in cotton clothes worn through.

Though life can often fray us, leaving only threadbare seams,
Autumn eyes remind us of what our lives have been.

Craig Smith
October 2025

71

Autumn Eyes

Autumn Eyes

Made in the USA
Columbia, SC
30 November 2025

74467267R00049